ABANDONED
CIVILISATIONS

ABANDONED CIVILISATIONS

The Mysteries Behind More Than 90 Lost Worlds

Kieron Connolly

amber
BOOKS

Published by
Amber Books Ltd
United House
North Road
London N7 9DP
United Kingdom
www.amberbooks.co.uk
Instagram: amberbooksltd
Facebook: www.facebook.com/amberbooks
Twitter: @amberbooks

ISBN: 978-1-78274-667-6

Project Editor: Michael Spilling
Designer: Andrew Easton
Picture Research: Justin Willsdon

Printed in China

Contents

Introduction

Temples hidden deep in the jungle, cities half-buried in desert sands, colossal slabs of ancient monuments scattered carelessly on the ground – images like these are bound to make us wonder: how could such mighty civilizations have collapsed? As we shall see in *Abandoned Civilizations*, the reasons can be manifold, from climate change and environmental damage to invasions and religious conflict, as well as shifting patterns of trade.

Often with the disintegration of ancient societies, the grandiose edifices were looted and nature was free to eradicate all but the most robust structures. Yet, sometimes, nature has proved to be the protector. From Africa to India to Mexico, there are citadels and temples where the jungle or the desert cocooned magnificent structures for hundreds of years, shielding them not just from the elements, but from humankind, too. Rediscovered in the modern era, these places can be newly explored. We cannot explain all their mysteries – that is part of their appeal – but we can begin to understand how they were lost and are now found again.

ABOVE:
Timgad, Batna, Algeria
Roman Timgad was lost beneath the desert for more than a millennium, but the sand preserved the city, too. It was not rediscovered until the 19th century.

RIGHT:
My Son, Quang Nam, Vietnam
The Champa Kingdom built Hindu temples at their capital My Son in central Vietnam from the fourth–14th centuries CE. By the early 15th century, though, My Son had been lost to the Viet, followers of Confucianism, invading from the north.

Africa

In surveying wide spans of history, we are at risk of telescoping the distant past and treating centuries and whole millennia as if they were a mere generation or two. When Julius Caesar built the city of Carthage in north Africa in the first century BCE, the pyramids of Egypt were already 2,000 years old. They were as old to Caesar as he is to us. Even to some of the pharaohs, the pyramids must have appeared ancient: to build the Valley of the Kings between the 16th and 11th centuries BCE, the Egyptians of the New Kingdom looted the pyramids of the Old Kingdom – which had been constructed 1,000 years earlier.

Egyptian civilization, of course, went back even further than that. Uniting the desert of the lower Nile Valley in 3100 BCE, the first kingdom built its wealth on the grain grown after the Nile flooded its banks each year. But if we go back further still, we see a different north Africa, with cave paintings in Algeria and Tunisia from the seventh millennium BCE depicting elephants, giraffes and rhinoceroses, showing clearly that the region wasn't always a desert. In fact, it once had the climate of the savannah. Future civilizations might witness it becoming grassland again, and regard all its years in the desert as ancient history.

LEFT:
The Great Temple, Abu Simbel, Aswan Governorate, Egypt
The twin temples at Abu Simbel were carved out of a mountainside during the reign of Pharaoh Ramesses II (1279–1213 BCE). Lost for millennia beneath the shifting desert sands, they weren't discovered until archaeological excavations in the early 19th century. When, in the 1960s, the construction of the Aswan High Dam put the temples at risk of being flooded, they were dug out in their entirety and reassembled on higher ground.

Tin Tazarift, Tassili n'Ajjer, Algeria

The Sahara may be a desert today, but it once had the climate of the African savannah and the 15,000 cave paintings and engravings at Tassili n'Ajjer (6000 BCE to the first centuries CE) depict not just hunters, sheep and herds of cattle, but elephants, giraffes and rhinoceroses. One of the oldest artworks at the site, this fresco shows a stylized round-headed hunter decorated with feathers. In the far right, a hunter's bow can be seen.

Made around 6000 BCE, the rock
engravings and cave paintings at
Wadi Mathendous include images
of elephants, giraffes, wildcats,
crocodiles, hippopotamuses,
aurochs (extinct cattle) and a
human figure killing a rhinoceros.

Twyfelfontein, Kunene Region, Namibia

At Twyfelfontein there are more than 2,500 engravings and paintings dating from the fourth millennium to the first century BCE. Made by hunter-gatherers who inhabited the semi-desert environment, most of the artworks depict animals such as antelopes and kudus. This piece is unusual in that it depicts human figures.

Twyfelfontein, Kunene Region, Namibia

The lion at the bottom of the painting has an elongated tail with what looks like a pawmark at the tip. It is suggested that this represents a human transformed into a lion in the spirit world. Similarly, the giraffe appears to have five horns. Other animals in the painting include antelope.

ABOVE AND LEFT:

Laas Geel, Hargeisa, Somalia
Dated as very broadly from a time
between 9000 and 3000 BCE, the
Laas Geel rock art is found in ten
granite alcoves and overhangs.
The paintings depict herders, a
giraffe, dogs and, as seen here,
long-horned cattle that seem to be
wearing ceremonial robes.

ALL PHOTOGRAPHS:

The Pyramid of Cheops, Giza, Egypt

Egyptologists generally believe that the largest of the three pyramids at Giza, the Pyramid of Cheops, was built between c. 2580 and 2560 BCE as a tomb for Pharaoh Khufu.

Standing 146.5 metres (481ft) tall, the pyramid was for almost 4,000 years the tallest structure in the world. Originally it was covered in smooth white limestone, but what we see today is the underlying granite core.

Still being explored, the purpose of all its passages and chambers is not fully understood.

The Sphinx, Giza, Egypt
Cut out of the limestone bedrock, the Sphinx is generally believed to have been constructed by the Pharaoh Khafre (c. 2558–2532 BCE), who also built the second pyramid at Giza. The monument has the body of a lion and a human head, which is thought to represent Khafre himself. Close to the Egyptian Old Kingdom capital at Memphis, the Sphinx forms part of the Giza necropolis complex of pyramids, monuments and cemeteries.

ALL PHOTOGRAPHS:

Waset, Luxor, Egypt

The ruins of Waset (Thebes) are found today within the modern city of Luxor. Located 644km (400 miles) up the River Nile from Memphis, Waset was the capital of Egypt during the New Kingdom (c. 1550 – c. 1077 BCE).

Built during the reign of Pharaoh Amenhotep III (1388–1350 BCE), the Luxor Temple (above) is dedicated to the rejuvenation of kingship.

Rams at the Temple of Karnak (right) – Amun, the local deity, was identified with the Ram.

Pillars support the portico in the courtyard of the Temple of Ramesses III (opposite).

PREVIOUS PAGES:

The Great Temple, Abu Simbel, Aswan Governorate, Egypt
Four 20-metre (66ft) high sandstone statues of Ramesses II decorate the façade of the Great Temple at Abu Simbel. Damaged in an earthquake soon after its construction (estimated to be 1265–44 BCE), the head and torso of one of the statues now lie at its feet. The temple having fallen into disuse, by the sixth century BCE the desert sands had already risen up as far as the knees of the statues.

LEFT:

The Great Temple, Abu Simbel, Aswan Governorate, Egypt
Inside the Great Temple are three rooms decreasing in size from the entrance to the sanctuary. In the hypostyle hall, the eight pillars represent a deified Ramesses. On its walls, the bas-reliefs feature many battle scenes, including Ramesses riding a war chariot against the Hittites during the Battle of Kadesh (1274 BCE). On just two days of the year, the first rays of the rising sun penetrate the whole length of the temple, illuminating the sanctuary on the far wall.

OVERLEAF:

The statues at the feet of Ramesses II represent his mother, his chief wife Nefertari and his children. Ramesses, who led successful military campaigns against Syria and into Nubia in the south, built extensively and monumentally across Egypt – at Abu Simbel in the south, at Luxor in Upper Egypt, and in the Nile Delta, where he constructed Pi-Ramesses, his new capital.

Nubian Pyramids, Meroë, Sudan
A former colony of the Egyptian
Empire, the Kushite Kingdom was
established on the River Nile in
the eighth century BCE. It lasted
until the early fourth century CE,
when the collapse of trade with
neighbouring states and a draining
military conflict with the Roman
Empire brought about its end.
Meroë, the kingdom's final capital
(c. 300 BCE – c. 300 CE), was a centre
of iron and gold production. These
granite and sandstone pyramids,
of which there are 200, were burial
tombs for kings and queens.

Antonine Baths, Carthage, Tunis Governorate, Tunisia
The Antonine Baths are from Roman Carthage, which was begun by Julius Caesar in 49 BCE. But the Roman city was built on the ruins of Phoenician Carthage, a major port and city state that Rome had destroyed in 146 BCE. In 698 CE, Carthage was conquered by the Umayyad Caliphate. Its walls were torn down, its water supply cut off and its harbours made unusable.

Timgad, Batna Province, Algeria
Founded by the Roman emperor
Trajan in 100 CE, Timgad was
built as a military colony to
defend against the Berbers of the
Aures Mountains. On expansion,
the city gained numerous baths,
an amphitheatre, a library and
basilica, becoming a centre of early
Christianity. With the incursion of
Germanic tribes into the Roman
Empire in the fifth century, the city
was sacked by the Vandals, before
later also coming under attack
from the Berbers. When Byzantine
forces entered Timgad a century
later, they found it empty. Under
Byzantine rule, the city revived,
but, after an Arab invasion in
the eighth century, it was again
abandoned.

Gradually buried beneath
the desert, Timgad was lost for
more than a millennium before
archaeologists discovered the tip
of Trajan's Arch in the late 19th
century, leading to the uncovering
of the rest of the city.

ALL PHOTOGRAPHS:

Great Citadel, Great Zimbabwe, Masvingo Province, Zimbabwe

The Great Zimbabwe area was settled by the fourth century CE but construction of the stone walls, steps and buildings seen here did not begin until the 11th century. Spanning 730 hectares (1800 acres), the site was inhabited by descendants of the Gokomere people – ancestors of the Shona of southern Africa today. Its importance was built on locally mined gold and far-reaching trade: Chinese pottery and Arab coins have been found in the excavations.

The oldest part of Great Zimbabwe, the Hill Complex (right), stands on a granite rock high above the surrounding plain. It was occupied from the ninth to the 13th centuries. A later construction, the Great Enclosure (far right), has 11m (36ft) high walls extending 250m (820ft), making it the largest ancient structure south of the Sahara Desert. For unknown reasons, the settlement declined after 1450. Great Zimbabwe is not unique. There are similar but smaller sites elsewhere in Zimbabwe and Mozambique.

Asia

The discovery of an ancient temple or a whole city entwined in reeds and lost in the jungle might sound like a scene from a movie, but such moments don't only exist in fiction. Before being abandoned, the temples in the caves at Ajanta in India were last painted in the fifth century CE. Overgrown, although not entirely forgotten by local people, it wasn't until the 19th century – 1,400 years later – that the caves were fully explored. Nor is Ajanta the only case: before rediscovery in the 1800s, the temples at Khajuraho – also in India – had been left to the jungle for 600 years, while in Indonesia the temple at Borobudur had been abandoned since the 14th century.

More famous than all these is Angkor in Cambodia. Although never completely lost in the jungle, this vast city had been abandoned for more than two centuries and was wildly overgrown when French archaeologists began to explore it in the 1860s.

Jungle can be so dense that a building just a few metres away could be thoroughly obscured by foliage. Who knows what ancient, hidden delights we might yet stumble across in the jungles of the world?

LEFT:
Ta Prohm Temple, Angkor, Siem Reap, Cambodia
Founded in the late ninth century and abandoned as the capital of the Khmer Empire in 1431, Angkor was once the most extensive city in the world, its temples, houses, canals and rice paddies stretching across a 1,000-square-km (390-square-mile) area. Its wooden secular buildings have not survived, but 1,000 sandstone temples remain.

LEFT AND ABOVE:

Bhimbetka, Madhya Pradesh, India

With paintings dating back 30,000 years, Bhimbetka's 243 caves contain the earliest traces of human life in the whole of the Indian subcontinent. Although the caves were known about, it was only in the late 19th century that they attracted academic interest.

This painting, which shows armed soldiers on horseback, dates from 1000–800 BCE. Other cave paintings at Bhimbetka feature animals, such as bison, elephants, tigers, rhinoceroses and deer, as well as hunting scenes, sky chariots and depictions of tree gods. The colours on the rock art were created from vegetable and mineral dyes.

39

Satkunda, Madhya Pradesh, India
In India there are more than 1,000 rock shelters containing cave paintings across 150 sites, but the highest concentration is found in sandstone caves in Madhya Pradesh. This site, 24 km (15 miles) from the city of Bhopal, has cave art dating back 5,000 years. The scene shows warriors on horseback.

Mohenjo-daro, Sindh, Pakistan
Built around 2500 BCE, the city at Mohenjo-daro was one of the major settlements of the Indus Valley Civilization, which stretched from what is today northeast Afghanistan, through Pakistan to northwest India.

Indicating sophisticated urban planning, Mohenjo-daro was laid out on a grid system with brick buildings. The citadel, visible in the distance, included public baths, a drainage system and underground heating.

It is not known for certain why the Indus Valley Civilization collapsed, but scholars suggest that drought was one cause: around 1800 BCE the monsoon weakened, leaving the climate cooler and drier. Within a century, most of the cities, including Mohenjo-daro, had been abandoned, their populations moving east to the Ganges River basin.

Chogha Zanbil, Khuzestan Province, Iran

Built about 1250 BCE by the Elamite king Untash-Napirisha, the complex at Chogha Zanbil was centred around this mud-brick ziggurat – a sacred, rectangular, stepped building. Beyond the ziggurat were 11 lesser temples, royal palaces and a sophisticated refinery for filtering water channelled in from the Choaspes River. The five-stepped ziggurat would originally have been topped with a temple that reached 53m (174ft) high: today it only stands at half that height. Glazed terracotta statues of bulls and winged griffins once guarded the entrance.

The site was destroyed by the Assyrian king Ashurbanipal in 640 BCE.

LEFT:

Persepolis, Fars Province, Iran
A complex of monumental
stairways, grand approaches,
vast throne rooms and hundreds
of sculpted friezes, Persepolis
was founded by Darius I in 515
BCE as the Achaemenid Empire's
ceremonial capital.

At its peak under Darius I, the
Achaemenid Empire was the largest
that had ever existed, stretching
from the Mediterranean and Black
Sea in the west to the Indus Valley
in the east. In 334 BCE, Alexander
III of Macedon – Alexander the
Great – invaded Asia Minor,
defeating Darius III's Persian
forces in a series of battles and
conquering Babylon and Susa, the
empire's true capitals.

When Persepolis surrendered
in 330 BCE, Alexander's forces
looted the city before setting it
on fire. Soon after, Darius III was
murdered, the Achaemenid Empire
disintegrated and Alexander
continued his advance eastwards,
making Persepolis and his other
conquests provinces of the
Macedonian Empire.

OVERLEAF:

Persepolis, Fars Province, Iran
This limestone relief from the
Apadana – the largest hall at
Persepolis – shows delegates from
the subject nations of the Persian
Empire queuing to pay tribute to
Darius I. Art was mirroring life:
the Apadana would have been
used by kings to receive delegates
paying tribute.

The Terracotta Army, Shaanxi, China

Discovered by farmers digging a well in 1974, the Terracotta Army collection includes sculptures of more than 8,000 life-size soldiers, 130 chariots and 150 cavalry horses buried in the necropolis of Qin Shi Huang, the first emperor of China, who died in 210 BCE.

Designed to protect the emperor in the afterlife, the figures, which were originally painted in bright colours, also include officials, musicians and acrobats. In the two millennia after the tomb was completed, up to 5 metres (19ft) of soil had amassed on the site.

Still under excavation, the immense necropolis, which is modelled on the Qin capital Xianyang, measures 98 square km (38 square miles).

RIGHT:

Ajanta Caves, Aurangabad District, Maharashtra, India

Carved out of flood basalt rock on a bend in the Waghur River, the Ajanta Caves include Buddhist rock-cut sculptures and paintings dating from two very separate phases: the first beginning in the second century BCE, the second between 460 and 480 CE.

Over the centuries, the 29 caves fell into disuse and the entrances became obscured by jungle. Although known about locally, it was not until the caves were brought to the attention of the British colonial administration in the early 19th century that they began to be explored.

OVERLEAF:

Cave 26, Ajanta Caves, Aurangabad District, Maharashtra, India

A worship hall, Cave 26 was dug out in the late fifth century CE, the second phase of construction at Ajanta. At the centre is a rock-cut stupa showing a seated Buddha. Other artworks in the cave include a reclining Buddha and depictions of scenes from his life.

ALL PHOTOGRAPHS:

Jiaohe, Xinjiang Uygur Autonomous Region, China

Situated in far northwest China, Jiaohe was an important city on the Silk Road from the end of the second century BCE up until the city's destruction at the hands of the Mongols in the 13th century. Its houses were dug into the ground and its bricks were made with dried mud.

Falling under the rule of the Tang Dynasty in 640 CE, Jiaohe was, for a while, the headquarters of the Tang Dynasty's Western Army. Despite its military role, the city had no walls – its location, on a leaf-shaped cliff between two steep river valleys, provided a natural fortress.

Niya, Xinjiang Uygur Autonomous Region, China
Located in the Taklamakan Desert, it is believed that Niya was once a commercial centre on the southern branch of the Silk Road. The city peaked between 500 and 1000 CE, but why it was abandoned is unknown. Once deserted, Niya was lost beneath the desert sands and not rediscovered until the early 20th century.

Stone City, Tashkurgan County, Xinjiang Uygur Autonomous Region, China

Today the city walls are all that remain of Stone City, but, marking the western junction of Silk Road routes across the Taklamakan Desert, it was an important settlement for centuries. Repeatedly expanded until the 14th century, during the late Qing Dynasty (1644–1912) a new city was built to the south and Stone City was abandoned.

Reclining Buddha, Mogao Caves, Gansu, China

Buddhism entered China from the west, with monks following the Silk Road from Central Asia introducing it in the first century CE. Having crossed the Taklamakan Desert, they established a community at Dunhuang, and, seeking somewhere nearby to meditate, began carving out the caves at Mogao.

The earliest surviving caves date from the Sixteen Kingdoms (366–439 CE), with the most recent being completed a millennium later, during the Yuan Dynasty (1227–1368). At its height, there were more than 1,000 caves at Mogao, of which 735, containing extensive murals and 2,400 clay sculptures, remain. This 15.6 metre (51ft) reclining Buddha was made in the late eighth or early ninth century when Dunhuang was under Tibetan occupation.

Following the fall of the Tang Dynasty in the early 10th century, after which China shifted to favouring trade by sea routes rather than the Silk Road as Islam spread across Central Asia, Dunhuang fell into decline. Investment in the caves trailed off and Mogao remained a destination for only the most devout.

Some of the caves had been blocked off by sand when interest was renewed in the late 19th century. In one cave, sealed since the 11th century, up to 50,000 manuscripts were found. Containing many works on Buddhism, the collection included a Chinese version of the Diamond Sutra, which, dating from 868 CE, is the oldest known dated printed book. In the collection were also Nestorian Christian manuscripts, as well as works from the Chinese government and dictionaries.

Naqsh-E Rajab, Fars Province, Iran
The sculptures cut into the limestone at Naqsh-E Rajab date from the early Sasanian Empire in the third century CE. This bas-relief commemorates Shapur I's (241–272 CE) victory in 244 CE over the Romans. It shows Shapur on horseback, followed by his sons and nobles.

ALL PHOTOGRAPHS:
Sigiriya, Central Province, Sri Lanka

The history of Sigiriya is uncertain, but this is one version: in 477 CE, Kasyapa, the illegitimate son of King Dhatusena, staged a coup, murdering his father and seizing the throne from his elder brother, Moggallana. Moving the capital of Sri Lanka from Anuradhapura to Sigiriya, Kasyapa built his palace fortress on the 180 metre (590ft) high granite rock.

Today only the Lion Gate's paws (far left) – cut out of the rock itself – remain, but above them once stood a sculpture of a lion's head. Sigiriya had more than 100 ponds (above) at the palace and in the grounds in the valley below. Built close to the summit of the rock, this is believed to have been the king's bathing pond.

The palace walls feature frescoes (left) of more than 500 women, though whom they represent is not known.

Sigiriya, Central Province, Sri Lanka
Having fled to India, Moggallana raised an army and returned to defeat his younger brother Kasyapa in battle in 495 CE. With his armies deserting him, Kasyapa, according to one account, committed suicide. When Moggallana moved the capital back to Anuradhapura, Sigiriya continued in a diminished capacity as a Buddhist monastery until the 14th century.

Greater Kyz Kala, Soltangala, Merv, Turkmenistan

The Greater Kyz Kala was a Kushk, a semi-fortified, two-storey palace with distinctive corrugated walls.

Soltangala was the largest of the cities of Merv, an oasis site on the Silk Road in western Central Asia. Cities had existed at Merv since the third century BCE, but the construction of Soltangala was instigated in the mid-eighth century CE by the Persian-led Abbasid Revolution that toppled the Arab-led Umayyad Dynasty. Reflecting the greater influence of Central Asia in the Islamic Empire, the caliphate now began to look increasingly eastwards.

With the Abbasid Caliphate weaker in the 13th century, Soltangala's importance was already on the wane when, in 1221, invading Mongols butchered many of its inhabitants.

Bam Citadel, Kerman Province, Iran

The largest mud-brick building in the world, Bam Citadel dates from the Achaemenid Empire (550–330 BCE), though most of the construction work was made during the Parthian (247 BCE–224 CE) and Sasanian (224–651) empires. An important area for cotton and silk production, as well as being on the Silk Road, Bam was conquered by the Arabs in the seventh century and the Mongols in the 13th century. Over the centuries, the civilian population moved out of the citadel and into the new town built beyond its ramparts. By the late 19th century, no civilians were living in the citadel and, in 1932, the last garrison left.

In 2003 Bam was struck by a major earthquake that killed more than 26,000 people. Up to 90 per cent of the buildings in the area were damaged or, as in the case of the citadel, largely destroyed. Immense reconstruction work began and, by 2016, almost all of Bam Citadel had been rebuilt.

OVERLEAF:

Bagan, Mandalay, Myanmar

From the ninth to 13th centuries, Bagan was the capital of the Pagan Kingdom. At the kingdom's peak in its final two centuries, more than 10,000 temples, pagodas and monasteries were constructed. Buddhism became the dominant religion, but Hinduism and other local traditions were tolerated.

Repeated Mongol invasions in the late 13th century were, however, disruptive and the Pagan Kingdom eventually collapsed. Bagan survived, but only as a lesser settlement and pilgrimage destination.

ALL PHOTOGRAPHS:
Borobudur, Magelang, Central Java, Indonesia
Constructed in the ninth century CE during the reign of the Sailendra Dynasty, the Buddhist temple at Borobudur was abandoned in the 14th century following the conversion of Java to Islam.

A step pyramid structure, the temple has nine platforms: the lower six are square, the upper three are round. With more than 500 statues and more than 2,500 relief panels, Borobudur is the world's largest Buddhist temple. Pilgrims pass through the corridors and stairways, following narrative stone reliefs of Buddha's life as they ascend physically through the temple and metaphorically through the levels of Buddhist cosmology.

Borobudur, Magelang, Central Java, Indonesia
On the three circular upper platforms of Borobudur, a Buddha statue is seated inside each of 72 perforated stupas. Located in an elevated area between two volcanoes, the temple was hidden beneath volcanic ash and jungle until, in 1814, local Javanese brought the site to the attention of Thomas Stamford Raffles, the British Lieutenant-Governor of Java (1811–16).

LEFT AND ABOVE:

Prambanan, Central Java, Indonesia

Possibly built as a response by the Sanjaya Dynasty to the Buddhist temple at Borobudur, the Hindu temple complex at Prambanan was begun around 850 CE and expanded in the early 10th century. Originally containing 240 temples, it is the largest Hindu site in Indonesia.

After the court was moved to East Java in 929 CE – perhaps because of the eruption of nearby Mount Merapi or possibly due to a power struggle – Prambanan fell into decline. Then, during a major earthquake in the 16th century, the temples collapsed.

Under the short-lived British occupation of the Dutch East Indies (1811–16), a survey of the ruins was first commissioned, but it wasn't until the 20th century that the Dutch began reconstruction work on the main temples.

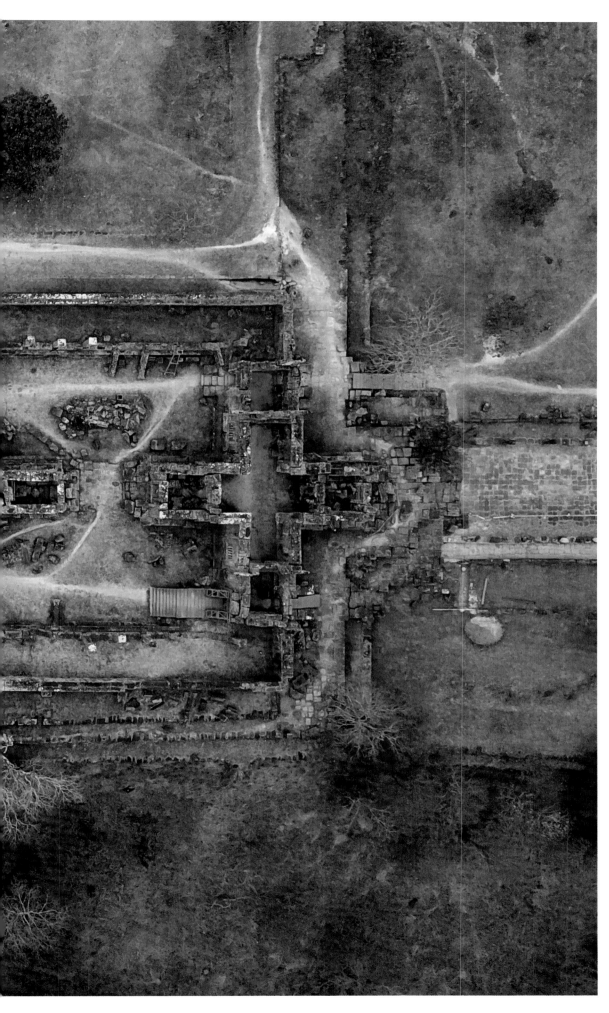

PREVIOUS PAGES:

Khajuraho, Madhya Pradesh, India

Isolation and neglect may have saved the Hindu and Jain temples at Khajuraho in central India. Largely built by the Chandela dynasty between 950 and 1050 CE, the 85 temples stretched over 21 square km (8 square miles) in hills 56km (35 miles) from the Chandela capital of Mahoba. When the Chandela Kingdom was seized by the Muslim forces of the Delhi sultanate in the 13th century, Khajuraho fell into decline.

Some temples were destroyed, but the remoteness of Khajuraho seems to have protected it from the complete desecration inflicted on other holy sites. Instead, as the centuries passed, the forests engulfed Khajuraho. Then, in 1838, locals led a British surveyor to the temples and they began to be explored again. With the vegetation now cut back, a tourist town has built up around Khajuraho.

The temples themselves, of which 22 survive, are known for their erotic sculptures, although these constitute only about 10 per cent of the panels. The others depict farming scenes, warriors, Hindu gods and Jain teachers.

LEFT:

Preah Vihear Temple, Preah Vihear, Cambodia

Situated on a cliff high in the Dangrek Mountains on what is today Cambodia's northern border with Thailand, Preah Vihear is a Hindu temple mainly built in the 11th and 12th centuries by the Khmer Empire. When Hinduism declined in the region, the temple was used by Buddhists.

From the early 14th century, the Khmer Empire began to decline. It has been suggested that this was caused by a number of factors, records showing, for instance, that monsoons became much more variable, with unusually heavy years of rainfall followed by droughts. Then there were invasions from the Ayutthaya Kingdom to the north, dynastic disputes within the empire, and, in converting from Hinduism to Buddhism, a weakening in the concept of the god-king, which, possibly, caused a falling off in support for royal authority.

LEFT:
Banteay Chhmar Temple, Banteay Meanchey, Cambodia
Not only neglected for years but looted, and, during Cambodia's civil war in the 1970s and 1980s, littered with mines, the Buddhist temple at Banteay has now been

partly restored. Built during the reign of Khmer king Jayavarman VII (1181–1218), its bas-reliefs depict military engagements, such as against the Champa of southern Vietnam, as well as scenes from daily life.

ABOVE AND OVERLEAF:
Angkor Wat, Siem Reap, Cambodia
On a site measuring 162.6 hectares (402 acres), Angkor Wat is the largest religious monument in the world. Built by Khmer king Suryavarman II in the first half of the 12th century, the temple was originally dedicated to the Hindu god Vishnu, but by the end of the century had been adapted for

Buddhist worship. The bas-relief above, as with most at Angkor Wat, depicts a scene from one of the Hindu epics.

Angkor was built with an elaborate grid of canals to collect, store and channel monsoon water for rice production. One theory about the decline of the city is that deforestation allowed soil to be dislodged when heavy rains fell, leading to the silting up of canals.

South Entrance, Angkor Thom, Siem Reap, Cambodia
Neighbouring Angkor Wat, Angkor Thom was founded by Jayavarman VII in the late 12th century. Covering an area of 9 sq km (3.5 sq miles), Angkor Thom's palaces and temples were sacked by the Ayutthaya Kingdom in 1431, after which point the Khmer capital was moved southeast. Falling into decline, the settlement at Angkor Thom was finally abandoned around 1660.

Lining a bridge over a moat into Angkor Thom, these Hindu deities are holding a *naga* (serpent), possibly representing the link between the secular world beyond and the divine world within.

ABOVE AND OPPOSITE:

Wat Mahathat, Ayutthaya, Thailand

Founded in 1351, the Ayutthaya Kingdom was a highly sophisticated society with trading links across Asia and, later, Europe. Its capital, the city of Ayutthaya, was built on an island in the Chao Phraya River, which flows into the Gulf of Thailand. At war with its neighbours, the kingdom attacked the Khmer Empire at Angkor to the southeast in the 15th century and from the mid-16th century fought repeated wars with the Burmese to the north.

In 1765, the Burmese again invaded the kingdom. Besieged, the city of Ayutthaya managed to hold out for 14 months before capitulating and being set on fire. This time the kingdom fell, but Burmese rule didn't last long: after a few months they had to withdraw to defend their own capital against a Chinese invasion.

Five years after the fall of Ayutthaya, a trading post 62km (40 miles) downstream was designated the new capital. It would become Bangkok.

The photograph (above) shows a stone Buddha head overgrown by a fig tree.

OVERLEAF:

The Great Wall, Luanping County, Hebei Province, China

Like most surviving parts of the Great Wall, the 10km (six miles) that make up the Jinshanling section were built during the Ming Dynasty (1368–1644). Largely unrepaired since 1570, the Jinshanling section is noted today for its many original features.

The first parts of the Great Wall were built as early as the seventh century BCE to protect China's northern border against raiding nomadic groups from the Eurasian steppe. Over the centuries, the walls were expanded and strengthened – brick and stone replacing earth and wood – while their function broadened to include border and trade control. Today the Ming section alone is 6,259km (3,889 miles) long.

With the annexation of Mongolia under the Qing Dynasty (1644–1912), China's borders moved and, no longer marking a frontier, construction and maintenance of the wall was discontinued.

Middle East

Where historians once believed that agriculture developed in the Middle East before being exported around the world, they now think that agriculture began independently in separate continents. In the Middle East from around 9000 BCE, wheat and goats were domesticated, followed by peas and lentils 1,000 years later, before the taming of horses by 4000 BCE. In China, rice, millet and pigs were domesticated around 7000 BCE; in South America, potatoes were cultivated and llamas tamed around 3500 BCE; in Central America, it was maize (corn) and beans around 4500 BCE. Around the globe, increased produce led to larger settlements, with the world's earliest large settlements emerging in the Middle East. From the fifth millennium BCE, cities with tens of thousands of inhabitants sprang up in the Fertile Crescent – the land that today reaches from Egypt through the Middle East and southern Turkey as far as western Iran. In the first millennium BCE, the Late Assyrian, Babylonian and Persian Empires ruled over millions of people. Later, the Roman Empire had 100 million subjects.

From a 9,000-year-old town in Turkey through to the magnificence of Petra and Palmyra, these pages tell the stories of some of the Fertile Crescent's most remarkable early civilizations.

LEFT:

Petra, Ma'an Governorate, Jordan

Geological patterns on sandstone caves. Founded in the fourth century BCE, the Nabatean city of Petra owed much of its wealth to the trade in frankincense. This aromatic resin was essential in religious rituals across the Middle East and the Mediterranean, while also being popular as far away as India and China. But it was the Nabateans, former nomads, who managed its collection in the desert. And it was through the oasis at Petra that any traders carrying frankincense north out of the desert had to pass – and pay a toll.

ALL PHOTOGRAPHS:

Catalhoyuk, Konya Province, Turkey

For 2.5 million years, humans had been hunter-gatherers, picking wild fruit and catching wild animals. But, from around 9500–8500 BCE, people in southeastern Turkey, western Iran and the Levant began to domesticate some local plant and animal species: wheat, barley, peas, lentils, sheep and cattle. Very gradually, seasonal and then permanent settlements evolved around these species – and the increase in food produced allowed the population to increase.

By 7000 BCE, the town of Catalhoyuk housed between 5,000 and 10,000 people, making it quite possibly the world's largest settlement at the time. Hunting was still a major source of food, but archaeological evidence shows that the people of Catalhoyuk had grain stores for wheat and barley, and kept sheep and some cattle.

Made of mud brick and clustered together, each house was entered from the roof, which was also the only form of ventilation. Without roads, rooftops were effectively streets.

The dead (above) were buried beneath the floors of the houses. Bodies were wrapped in reed mats and have been found with spinning whorls, axes and, in the case of this infant, stone beads.

PREVIOUS PAGES:

Uruk, Muthanna Governorate, Iraq
At its height in the early third millennium BCE, the walled city of Uruk was probably the largest city in the world, sustaining a population of 50,000–80,000 people. Located on the Euphrates River in southern Mesopotamia, the Sumerian city lost its dominance to Babylon around 2000 BCE. By 300 CE, it was mostly abandoned.

LEFT:

The Temple of the Obelisks, Byblos, Lebanon
Ranging from 50cm (20in) to 2.5m (8ft), there are 26 obelisks at this Phoenician temple from the early second millennium BCE. Among the obelisks were found 1,500 gold-covered votive offerings in the shape of human figures. In recent years, the temple has been moved by archaeologists to a new location to allow the excavation of an earlier temple beneath the original site.

ALL PHOTOGRAPHS:

Hattusa, Çorum Province, Turkey

Hattusa was the capital of the Hittite Empire, which in the second millennium BCE covered much of present-day Turkey, along with parts of northern Mesopotamia and the Levant. After the Hittite Empire was annexed by the Assyrians, Hattusa was overrun by invading forces – including the Phrygians from the Balkans – and burned to the ground. The kingdom's demise, however, is now seen more broadly as part of the Late Bronze Age collapse, where civilizations across the eastern Mediterranean – including Mycenae in Greece and the Egyptian Empire – disintegrated. Suggested causes for the collapse include climate change and drought, which led to crop failures and violent conflict between societies over resources.

(Right) A bas-relief showing Hittite gods of the Underworld.

(Below) A warrior god on the King's Gate.

(Far Right) Even after 3,000 years, this 70-metre (230-ft) long tunnel constructed from boulders is still passable.

Ain Dara, Afrin, Aleppo Governorate, Syria
In use from 1300–740 BCE, Ain Dara was a Syro-Hittite temple possibly
dedicated to the ancient Sumerian goddess Ishtar. Among its ruins
are basalt sculptures of lions and sphinxes, along with giant human
footprints carved into the stone floors. Ain Dara is noted for its similarity
to the Old Testament description of Solomon's Temple in Jerusalem.
In January 2018, the temple was badly damaged by Turkish airstrikes
against Kurdish forces during the Syrian Civil War.

Van Fortress, Van Province, Turkey
The Van Fortress was built by the Armenian kingdom of Urartu during the ninth to seventh centuries BCE. Overlooking the ruins of the Urartian capital of Tushpa, the lower part of the fortress is made from basalt, the upper part from mud bricks. Having risen in the ninth century BCE, the Urartian Empire was frequently in conflict with the Assyrians to the south, but eventually fell in the sixth century BCE to the Medes from Iran.

Ocean Necropolis, Myra, Antalya Province, Turkey
The Lycian rock-cut tombs in the town of Myra were originally painted bright red, yellow, blue and purple. They date from the fourth century BCE, when Lycia was part of the Macedonian Empire. Later a Roman protectorate, the rest of Myra is now largely lost beneath the flood plain of the River Myros, but its acropolis, theatre and baths have been excavated.

ALL PHOTOGRAPHS:

Petra, Ma'an Governorate, Jordan

Naturally defended in a mountain canyon, Petra developed at a crossroads on caravan routes in the desert. Despite the climate, the Nabateans, who settled here in the fourth century BCE, ingeniously managed to collect and channel enough spring water and rainwater to sustain, at the city's peak, a population of 30,000 people.

Rome made Petra a colony in the first century CE but when, in the following century, new maritime trade routes were established, and Palmyra in Syria emerged as a trading centre on the Silk Road, Petra's fortunes rapidly declined. This was exacerbated in 363 CE when an earthquake destroyed many of the city's buildings, along with its water conduit system.

(Above and overleaf) The first century CE Hellenistic amphitheatre, later modified by the Romans.

(Right) Petra's ruins include more than 800 tombs.

(Opposite) Carved out of the sandstone rockface, Al-Khazneh was a mausoleum and crypt built in the early first century CE. Although the façade is grandiose, the hall behind it is relatively small.

Masada, Judea, Israel
The fortress at Masada housed a Roman garrison until it was overcome by the Sicarii, a Jewish sect, during the Great Jewish Revolt in 66 CE. Fleeing persecution in Jerusalem, other Jews subsequently joined the Sicarii. Six years later, the Roman army besieged the fortress and over the course of three months built a ramp from which they launched an attack. We only have the account of historian Flavius Josephus to rely on, but, according to him, the Romans found that all 960 inhabitants of Masada – with the exception of two women hidden in a cistern – had committed mass suicide rather than surrender.

Great Colonnade, Palmyra, Homs Governorate, Syria
On the fringe of the Roman Empire, Palmyra was a mix of east and west: it looked like a Greco-Roman city, but its people worshipped local Semitic, Mesopotamian and Arab deities. Located at an oasis on trade routes across the Syrian Desert, Palmyra became a subject of Rome in the first century CE. The Great Colonnade was built over the following two centuries.

Valley of Tombs, Palmyra, Homs Governorate, Syria
There are more than 50 funerary monuments in the Valley of Tombs, the most recent of which dates from 128 CE.

Palmyra reached its peak in the 260s CE, when, rebelling against Roman rule, it established an empire across the Levant, Egypt and much of Asia Minor. But, in 273 CE, the Roman emperor Aurelian razed the city to the ground. It was rebuilt, but as a much smaller settlement, and further destruction by the Timurids in 1440 reduced Palmyra to a small village. During the Syrian Civil War in 2015, the ruins were occupied by Islamic State (IS), who sabotaged and destroyed many of the city's temples and buildings, while selling some artefacts to dealers.

ALL PHOTOGRAPHS:

Roman Theatre, Bosra, Dara'a, Syria

Constructed out of black basalt in the second century CE, the theatre at Bosra is one of the largest and best preserved Roman theatres in the whole empire. An agricultural area, Bosra was also a major junction on trade routes, particularly between Damascus and the Red Sea. Unusually, in the 13th century the Ayyubid Dynasty fortified the theatre and turned it into a citadel.

ALL PHOTOGRAPHS:

Temple Complex, Heliopolis, Baalbek, Lebanon

The temple complex of Heliopolis developed from the late first to the third century CE. Originally the site housed three temples to classical gods, but, during the Christianization of the Roman Empire in the fourth century, emperors ordered that two of the temples be replaced with churches.

Sacked by the caliph Marwan II in 748, the complex was abandoned. However, the Temple of Bacchus survived and today remains one of the empire's most richly adorned buildings.

Archway of Ctesiphon, Baghdad Governorate, Iraq
Once part of an imperial palace built in the third–sixth century CE, this is all that remains of Ctesiphon. The capital of the Parthian Empire (247 BCE–224 CE) and its successor, the Sasanian Empire (224–651 CE), Ctesiphon was ultimately abandoned in the eighth century CE when the Abbasid Caliphate built a new capital, Baghdad, just 35km (22 miles) away.

PREVIOUS PAGES:

Church of Saint Simeon Stylites, Aleppo Governorate, Syria

Consecrated in 475 CE, the Church of Saint Simeon Stylites was built around the pillar on which Saint Simeon had lived and preached for 37 years. Conquered during the Muslim conquest of Syria in the seventh century, the church had long been a ruin before it was further badly damaged by Russian airstrikes during the Syrian Civil War in 2016.

LEFT:

Grand Mosque, Harran, Sanliurfa, Turkey

The building of the Grand Mosque and its minaret predate Islam: constructed during Harran's Roman period, they were adapted for Islamic worship after the Arab conquest in the seventh century. Harran itself had been a major trading post as far back as the third millennium BCE. The city was destroyed by the Mongols in the 1260s.

Church ruins, Ani, Kars Province, Turkey

In the 10th and 11th centuries CE, Ani was the capital of the Bagratid Armenian kingdom, which stretched across most of present-day Armenia and eastern Turkey. Once sustaining a population of around 100,000 people, Ani was sacked by the Mongols in 1236 before being devastated by an earthquake in 1319. With that, it was reduced to a village and gradually abandoned.

Europe

The stone circles at Stonehenge in England, Newgrange in Ireland and Carnac in France largely remain a mystery to us. Alignments with solstices have been observed and burial sites found, but we can only hazard suggestions that these sites had ritual functions: though exactly what, we don't know.

In contrast, many of the entries in these pages are from Ancient Rome, about which we know a great deal. And yet, when we look at the ruins of Hadrian's Wall or the Colosseum in Rome, we may well wonder how such a mighty civilization came to fall. It is a question that historians have been asking for centuries – without reaching a definitive answer. Some suggest that plague and environmental exhaustion caused a population decline and a weakening of the economy; others that Christianity, which had been adopted as Rome's religion in the fourth century CE, undermined the empire. Some have argued that political infighting was the cause; others that the emergence of the Sassanid Persian Empire (226–651 CE) destabilised Rome. Another argument is that the invasions of Germanic tribes in the fourth and fifth centuries were prompted by the incursions of the Huns into Germanic lands.

LEFT:

The Parthenon, Athens, Attica, Greece

A temple, a church, a mosque – the Parthenon has been all of these, as over thousands of years Athens has passed through Greek, Roman, Byzantine and Ottoman hands. Built on the Acropolis in the fifth century BCE, the Parthenon was originally a temple dedicated to the goddess Athena. In the 17th century, it was partly destroyed in a bombardment by the Venetians.

Controversially, in 1801, Thomas Bruce, 7th Earl of Elgin, obtained a decree from the ruling Ottoman government to remove half of the Parthenon's marble sculptures. These he later sold to the British Museum in London, where they remain.

PREVIOUS PAGES:
Lascaux, Dordogne, France
Discovered in 1940, the cave
paintings at Lascaux are between
15,000 and 20,000 years old.
Alongside human figures and
abstract symbols, the paintings
include 900 images of animals, of
which more than 300 are horses, as
well as stags, cattle, bison, lions, a
bird and a bear. One painting of a
bull is 5.2 metres (17ft) long – the
largest depiction of an animal in
cave art.

LEFT:
Carnac, Brittany, France
There are more than 3,000 standing
stones in Brittany, most of which
are found in the village of Carnac.
Dating from around 3300 BCE –
though in some cases possibly as
early as 4500 BCE – the alignments
mainly consist of long rows of
menhirs, ranging from 4m (13ft)
tall down to 80cm (2ft 7in). At the
end of the rows are stone circles.

It is not known what purpose
or rituals the stones served, but it
has been suggested that they were
possibly aligned with the sunrise
and sunset, or with the stars.

ALL PHOTOGRAPHS:

Newgrange, County Meath, Ireland

Built c. 3200–3100 BCE, the monument at Newgrange consists of a circular stone and earth mound containing chambers that were possibly tombs. The only source of light is the opening above the doorway, which was aligned with the sunrise on the winter solstice. Forming a close ring outside the monument are kerbstones, many of which are decorated with megalithic art (above). Centuries later, a second ring of 12 standing stones (left and opposite) was made around the perimeter.

Stonehenge, Wiltshire, England
Believed to have been built in stages between 3000 and 2000 BCE, the stone circle at Stonehenge largely remains a mystery, both in how it was constructed and what purpose it served. The bluestones used for some of the circle were quarried 240km (150 miles) away in Wales. But, in an age before wheels, how were such immense stones transported so far?

Stonehenge is thought to be a site of importance in rituals, and it is known that around 2600 BCE the northeast entrance was modified, aligning it precisely with the winter solstice sunset and summer solstice sunrise at that time. Beyond the standing stones are several hundred ancient burial mounds.

Callanish I, Isle of Lewis, Outer Hebrides, Scotland

The largest of several stone circles, arcs and alignments on the Isle of Lewis, Callanish I was erected between c. 2900 and 2600 BCE. A monolith surrounded by a stone circle and five rows of standing stones, it seems to have been in use until around 1500–1000 BCE. At some time after the stones were put in place, a burial tomb was added. The purpose of Callanish I, though, is unknown.

RIGHT:

Avebury Stone Circles, Wiltshire, England

At Avebury, two stone circles are ringed by a larger stone circle, which itself is enclosed by a circular bank and ditch. An avenue of paired stones leads away from the edge of the bank. It is suggested that the construction happened in stages over many centuries from 3000–2400 BCE, beginning with the inner circles and working outwards. The site is believed to have had a function in rituals, although its exact purpose is not known.

LEFT AND ABOVE:
Knossos, Crete, Greece
The first high civilization
in Europe, the Minoans of
Crete colonised the eastern
Mediterranean between 2500
and 1450 BCE, their city at Knossos
becoming a ceremonial and
political centre. In attempting to
explain the reason for the end of
Minoan civilization, it has been
argued that the c. 1550–1500 BCE
volcanic eruption on the island
of Thera (present-day Santorini),
about 100km (60 miles) from
Crete, and the tsunami that it
triggered which devastated Minoan
ports, led to a long-term decline for
the Minoans. With the civilization
more vulnerable, the Minoans were
overcome by Myceneans invading
from the Greek mainland.

The Prince of the Lilies (above)
was reconstructed from three
fragments of fresco made in c.
1550 BCE. It shows a young man
with a necklace of lilies and a
crown of peacock feathers.

(Opposite) The alabaster chair
on the right has led archaeologists
to interpret this as a Throne Room.
Griffins are depicted on the wall
frescoes.

ALL PHOTOGRAPHS:

Magura, Vidin, Bulgaria

More than 750 images have been identified in the prehistoric cave art at Magura. Estimated to date from between 8000 and 1200 BCE, the images, painted in bat dung, include animals such as prehistoric goats, cattle, dogs and big birds. Human figures are shown hunting and dancing (above), as well as celebrating fertility rites and, it is believed, taking part in religious ceremonies. Other images show tools, plants, stars and geometrical shapes.

The detail (opposite) is thought to represent the Sun and forms part of what is considered to be a solar calendar.

Uffington White Horse, Oxfordshire, England
Dating from sometime between 1380 and 550 BCE, the Uffington White Horse was made by cutting 1m (3ft) deep trenches into the hillside and filling them with crushed white chalk. It has been debated whether the stylized figure does, in fact, represent a horse at all and not perhaps a dog or a sabre-toothed cat.

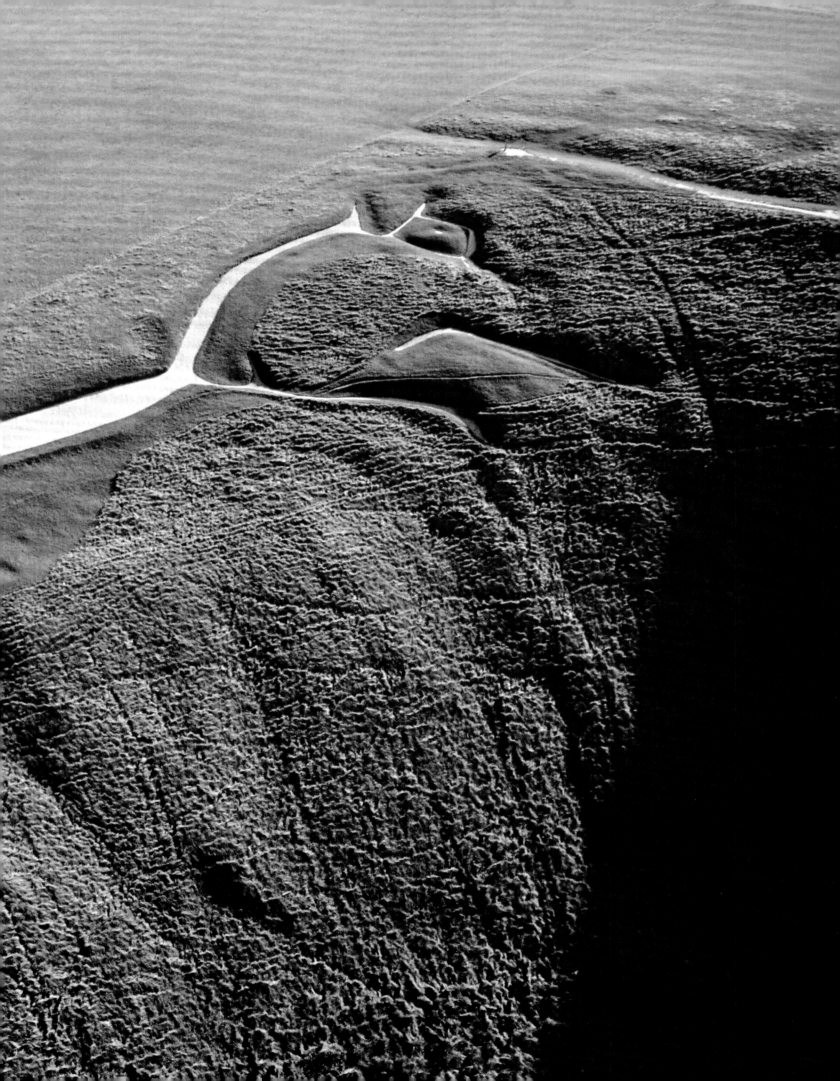

RIGHT:

Acropolis, Athens, Attica, Greece
The Acropolis had been inhabited since the fourth millennium BCE, but it was in the fifth century BCE that its major surviving buildings – the Parthenon, the Propylaia, the Erechtheion, the Temple of Athena Nike – were built. Commissioned by Athenian general Pericles, the construction project celebrated the Greek defeat of the Persian invasion of 479–50 BCE, during which Athens had been captured and the earlier Parthenon, along with other buildings, had been burnt down.

OVERLEAF:

Theatre, Delphi, Central Greece, Greece
From the seventh century BCE, high-ranking Greeks came to the town of Delphi to consult the Oracle, where, through the medium of a priestess in a trance, they believed the god Apollo would answer their questions.

Originally built in the fourth century BCE, Delphi's theatre was remodelled a number of times, including in preparation for Emperor Nero's visit in 67 CE. The town was abandoned in the sixth or seventh century.

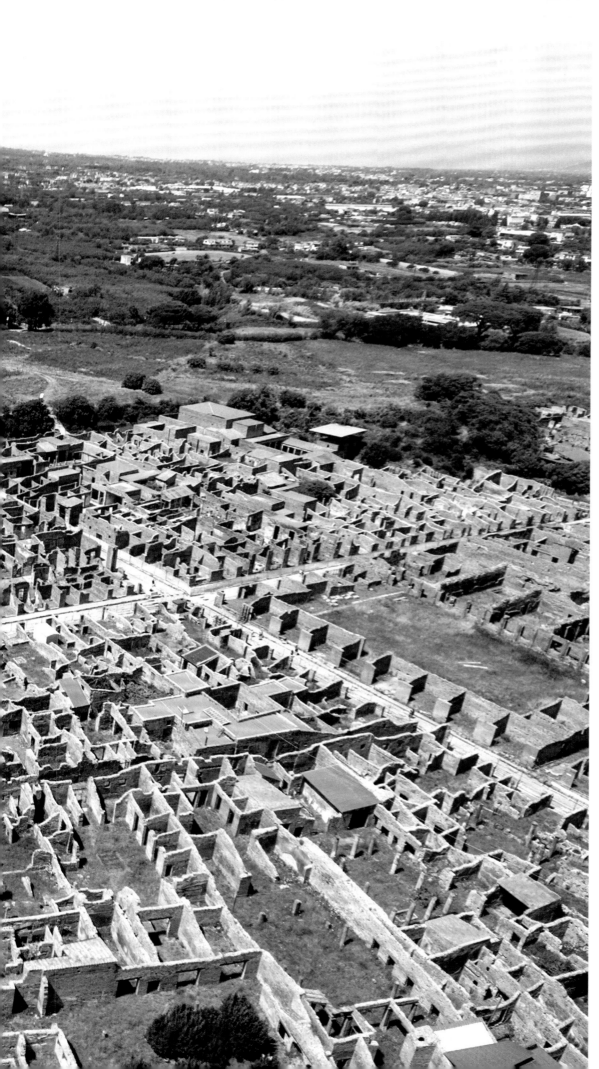

Pompeii, Campania, Italy
Once sustaining a population of around 11,000 people, Pompeii was a major Roman town until it was covered beneath 4–6m (13–20ft) of volcanic ash and pumice following the eruption of Mount Vesuvius (seen here in the distance) in 79 CE. Apart from the many villas and businesses, the town had two theatres and an amphitheatre.

ALL PHOTOGRAPHS:

Pompeii, Campania, Italy

Although the ash and pumice from the eruption of Mount Vesuvius buried Pompeii, it preserved it, too. First rediscovered in 1599 and properly excavated from 1748, the town, free from air and moisture for more than a millennium, was found to have many buildings and frescoes intact.

(Top) The people of Pompeii were most likely killed from the heat of the eruption rather than smothered by the volcanic ash. Over the centuries, their bodies disintegrated, leaving voids within the ash. To recreate the positions and shapes of the bodies, archaeologists injected plaster into those voids.

(Above) A replica of a statue of Apollo, outside the Temple of Apollo. The original statue was found in pieces in the early 19th century.

RIGHT:
Roman amphitheatre, Saintes, Nouvelle-Aquitaine, France
Almost 2,000 years after it was constructed and with its tiers now largely overgrown, the Roman amphitheatre in Saintes still holds performances, but today they are concerts rather than gladiatorial games. Saintes was founded by the Romans in c. 40 BCE and the amphitheatre, which could hold more than 12,000 spectators, was built c. 40 CE.

OVERLEAF:
Pula Arena, Pula, Istria, Croatia
Completed in 81 CE, the Roman amphitheatre at Pula held professional gladiatorial games until Emperor Honorius prohibited them in the sixth century. Combat between convicts and against wild animals, however, continued into the following century. The lowest tier of seats was for consuls, ambassadors, senators, priests and Vestal Virgins. Above them sat patricians, followed by plebeians and, on the top tier, women.

LEFT:

Catacombs, Rome, Italy
Cremation was originally the funerary custom among Romans, but Christians and Jews buried their dead. With the number of Christians in Rome increasing in the second century CE, large-scale catacombs were dug outside the city walls for burials. When Christianity became the state religion in the late fourth century, burials increasingly took place within church cemeteries and the use of catacombs declined.

ABOVE:

Colosseum, Rome, Italy
Made of stone and Roman concrete, the Colosseum was the largest amphitheatre ever built, holding an estimated 50,000–80,000 spectators. Completed in 80 CE, it held gladiatorial games, executions, re-enactments of battles and classical dramas into the sixth century.

During the Middle Ages, the base of the arena was used as a cemetery, vaulted spaces under the seating were converted into houses and workshops, and the marble façade was pulled down and burnt to make quicklime.

OVERLEAF:

Hadrian's Wall, England
At 117.5km (73 miles) long, Hadrian's Wall is the world's largest Roman artefact. Although it was said to have been built to defend the province of Britannia from the Ancient Britons to the north, its construction may have been more important as a broader expression of Roman power. Built between 122 and 128 CE, it is thought that the limestone wall was originally covered in plaster and painted white.

ABOVE:

Aqueduct, Segovia, Castile and Leon, Spain

The Roman aqueduct at Segovia brought water from the River Frio, 17km (11 miles) away. Completed in the late first or early second century, the aqueduct was partly destroyed when the Moors invaded in 1072 and Segovia was abandoned. The first reconstruction work was carried out under King Ferdinand and Queen Isabella in the late 15th to early 16th centuries.

OPPOSITE:

Aqua Claudia, Lazio, Italy

Mostly running underground, the Aqua Claudia aqueduct was 69km (43 miles) long, bringing spring water to Rome. Nearing the city, the aqueduct emerged on to arches, some of which are 30m (100ft) tall. Begun by Emperor Caligula in 38 CE, it was completed under his successor, Claudius, in 52 CE.

The Americas and the Pacific

The ancestors of the Maya, Inca and Native Americans in North, Central and South America crossed from Asia to Alaska at least 15,000 years ago. After that, unlike the exchange that happened over centuries between Africa, the Middle East, Europe and Asia through trade, migration and war, there was no further contact with the world beyond the Americas for thousands of years.

Considering this isolation, the number of similarities shared between the ancient civilizations of the Americas and the rest of the world is perhaps surprising. Rather like the Egyptians, the people of Teotihuacan in Mexico built monumental stone pyramids. Like the Romans, the Incas constructed extensive road networks and the Maya engineered canals. Like ancient Greece and medieval Persia, the Maya developed advanced mathematics and astronomy. Similar to the ancient Chinese, the Inca developed a counting system on knotted string, and the Maya created their own script.

Of course, what isolation had kept from the Americas were the viruses circulating in the rest of the world. When Europeans first made contact in the 15th and 16th centuries, it was largely disease, namely smallpox, that overwhelmed the native peoples and helped end the Maya and Inca civilizations.

LEFT:

Ollantaytambo, Cusco Region, Peru
Without steel or wheeled vehicles, without draft animals, and without a writing system, the Incas, between the early 15th and early 16th centuries, established a tightly organized society, produced monumental architecture and built an extensive road network. Ruling over 10–12 million people across what is today Peru, Ecuador and Bolivia, along with parts of Chile, Argentina and Colombia, they created possibly the largest empire in the world at the time.

Arnhem Land, Northern Territory, Australia
The Aboriginal cave art at Arnhem Land is about 28,000 years old, and is the oldest in Australia. Cave art in Arnhem Land depicts fish, wallabies, crocodiles, people and spiritual figures. Aboriginal people have lived in Australia for 45,000 years, after crossing by sea from the Indonesian archipelago.

177

Cave of Hands, Santa Cruz, Argentina

To create these outlines, the artists held one hand against the wall and blew paint over it. The cave paintings also include depictions of human figures in hunting scenes, rhea birds, guanacos (a species similar to llamas), as well as geometric patterns. From the bone-made pipes used to spray the paint, the artworks have been dated to between 11,000 and 7500 BCE.

Caral, Barranca, Peru
The largest of 30 settlements in the Norte Chico civilization – the oldest in the Americas – Caral was inhabited from c. 2600 to c. 2000 BCE. Located 12 miles (20km) from the coast, Caral was situated in an arid valley, which its people irrigated to grow crops and cotton. The city's ruins include six monumental stone pyramid structures, earthwork platform mounds and sunken plazas.

Nazca Lines, Ica, Peru

Visible from the surrounding foothills, these lines were made by members of the Nazca culture sometime between 200 and 600 CE. Although their purpose remains a mystery, the construction of the lines was simple: by removing the reddish surface stones to a depth of 10–15cm (4–6in), the white soil beneath was revealed. This Nazca line is thought to represent a pair of hands.

ALL PHOTOGRAPHS:

Nazca Lines, Ica, Peru

In an area of nearly 500 square km (190 square miles), there are 300 Nazca lines, the largest of which is a 285-metre (935ft) pelican. The majority of the drawings are of geometric shapes, such as triangles and spirals.

Approximately 90 of the lines depict the natural world, from plants, flowers and trees (above) to animal species, including a man, a monkey, a dog, a whale and birds, such as a condor (left).

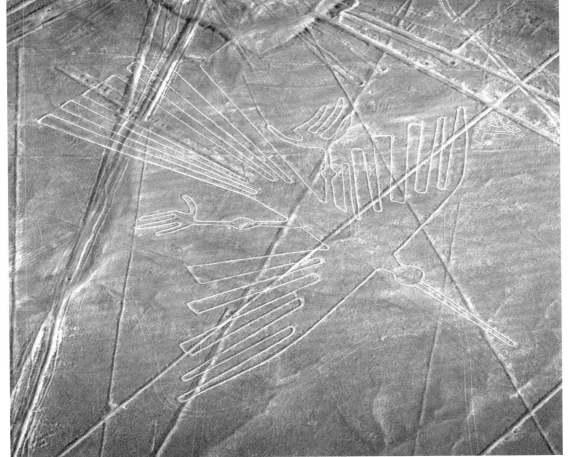

PREVIOUS PAGES:
Gate of the Sun, Lake Titicaca, La Paz, Bolivia
The Gate of the Sun was constructed from a solid piece of stone by the Tiwanaku Culture, which existed around Lake Titicaca from 300 to 1150 CE. This frieze above the doorway is thought to represent a Sun god. He is surrounded by winged effigies, some with human heads, the rest with the heads of condors.

LEFT:

Teotihuacan, State of Mexico, Mexico
Reaching its zenith with an estimated population of almost 250,000 people in 450 CE, Teotihuacan was the largest urban centre in the pre-Columbian Americas and the sixth largest city in the world. Covering a 83 square km (32 square mile) site, the city dominated the Valley of Mexico and was a centre of agriculture, trade and industry, mining obsidian (a volcanic glass) to produce knives and other tools. It interacted politically and culturally with the Maya civilizations in the Yucatan peninsula to the southeast.

The largest pyramid, the Pyramid of the Sun (in the foreground), was completed around 200 CE, but the earliest buildings date back to around 200 BCE. Laid out in a precise grid system, Teotihuacan had rows of houses, mansions and vast plazas, while the tops of the pyramids were reserved for rituals, including human sacrifice.

In around 550 CE, the city's major monuments were sacked and burned, but it is not known by whom. Teotihuacan was abandoned around the year 750.

ALL PHOTOGRAPHS:
Temple of the Feathered Serpent, Teotihuacan, State of Mexico, Mexico
Constructed between 150 and 200 CE, Teotihuacan's third largest pyramid is known today as the Temple of the Feathered Serpent because of the repeated representations (above and left) of that Mesoamerican deity. During the city's prime, the pyramids and other major buildings were painted red. Beneath the pyramid, evidence of human sacrifice was uncovered: the remains of 200 men and women were found with their hands tied behind their backs.

ABOVE:

Yaxchilan, Chiapas, Mexico
The Maya site at Yaxchilan is
known today for its seventh and
eighth century buildings, which
feature well-preserved sculptures
and stelae depicting the dynastic
history of the city. This sculpture
on a doorway shows a leader
carrying a ceremonial staff.

RIGHT:

Calakmul, Campeche, Mexico
One of the largest Maya cities,
Calakmul reached its peak in
the seventh century CE, when its
population is estimated to have
been about 50,000. Apart from its
immense pyramids, there are more
than 6,500 ancient structures in the
city's ruins, including aqueducts,
reservoirs, ballgame courts, royal
burial tombs, and causeways
connecting the city-state to satellite
towns. Calakmul's main rival state
– against which it occasionally
went to war – was Tikal, 100km
(60 miles) to the south.

Tikal, El Peten, Guatemala
Like the other major buildings
at Tikal, the largest pyramid
(right), is aligned with the Sun and
stars, indicating that at that time
the Maya had a more advanced
understanding of astronomy than
their European contemporaries.
They also developed advanced
mathematics and the Maya script.

Maya urban centres had
developed by the late second
century BCE and peaked between
the third and early 10th centuries.
Across what is today southeastern
Mexico, all of Guatemala and
Belize, and parts of El Salvador
and Honduras, the Maya built city-
states with pyramids, sophisticated
irrigation systems and elaborate
sculptures, while having no metal
tools, beasts of burden or wheels.

By the end of the 10th century,
Tikal and other Maya city-states
had been abandoned, possibly
as a result of overpopulation,
drought and crop failure caused
by soil exhaustion. Although not
completely forgotten by locals,
Tikal was left to be absorbed by
the jungle until it was explored in
the 1850s.

Copan, Copan, Honduras
A detail from a doorway
constructed in the early eighth
century CE. It is thought that
the skull-like figure represents
ancestors living in the Underworld.
When the Maya city-state of
Copan collapsed in the ninth
century, the population ebbed away
and villagers stole the stones from
the monumental architecture to
build simple houses.

Palenque, Chiapas, Mexico
Palenque's Temple of the Inscriptions (far right) was a funerary monument to K'inich Janaab' Pakal, who rejuvenated the Maya city-state during his reign in the seventh century. Sculptures on the top level were originally colourful, with gods marked out in blue and the Underworld figures in yellow, all set against a light red background.

ALL PHOTOGRAPHS:

Palenque, Chiapas, Mexico

We know precisely when in the seventh and eighth centuries the various wings of the Palace were completed because Palenque's architects inscribed completion dates in the Maya calendar on the walls (left and opposite).

Human sacrifice was practised throughout the Maya civilization. Enemy kings would be decapitated; other victims were disembowelled or had their hearts removed. Some had their hands tied to their feet and were rolled down temple steps. In order to provide a dead nobleman with some company at Palenque, a young woman was entombed alive.

After 800 CE, there was no new ceremonial construction at Palenque. An agricultural population remained, but gradually the city was abandoned. Although 90 percent of the Maya population disappeared after 800 CE, the Maya did survive – their language is still spoken today – but the civilization's larger settlements had collapsed.

LEFT AND ABOVE:

Chan Chan, La Libertad Region, Peru

The largest mud-brick city in the Americas, Chan Chan was the capital of the Chimor Kingdom, which ruled Peru's northern coast from c. 850 to c. 1470 CE. One of the most advanced American cultures before European contact, Chimor is known for its metalworking and black-stained ceramics. In the 1470s, the kingdom was conquered by the Incas. Sixty years later, though, the Inca Empire itself was conquered by Spaniard Francisco Pizarro. Still a source of riches, Chan Chan was looted by the Spanish. Pizarro went on to build the city of Trujillo just a few miles to the east of Chan Chan, further eclipsing the former Chimor capital. All the reliefs in the city reflect its coastal life: depictions include fish, waves, fishing nets and pelicans (above).

PREVIOUS PAGES:

Ciudad Perdida, Magdalena, Colombia

Believed to have been abandoned during the Spanish Conquest in the 16th century, the town now referred to as Ciudad Perdida ('Lost City') was probably founded around 800 CE. Lost in the jungle until 1972, the settlement consists of tiled roads, circular plazas and 169 terraces carved into the mountainside. Possibly a centre of the Tairona, it is thought that Ciudad Perdida once sustained a population of 2,000–8,000 people.

Tucume, Lambayeque, Peru
There are 26 pyramids and mounds at Tucume, a 220-hectare (540-acre) site inhabited by the Sican (800–1350), before being taken over by the Chimu (1350–1450), and lastly occupied by the Incas (1450–1532). The Sican built mud-brick monumental mounds as burial sites for the elite and places of worship.

Easter Island, Pacific Ocean, Chile

Easter Island's civilization didn't completely collapse, but when Europeans first made contact in 1722, they were presented with a mystery. They found 887 imposing stone statues – almost all of which had been toppled – and a poor society that no longer had the means to erect such huge structures. What had happened? Settled by Polynesians some time between 700 and 1,000 CE, it is believed that Easter Island's population had peaked at about 15,000 people in the early 17th century, before rapidly falling to below 3,000 as a result of environmental deterioration.

By the 18th century, the once forested island no longer had any tall trees nor the soil in which to grow them. Lack of tree species meant no nesting sites for the island's bird species, which died out. Deforestation meant that no new canoes for fishing could be built, while soil erosion led to poorer crops. Both animal and plant species also died out, it is suggested, due to the unintended introduction of the Polynesian rat.

Mesa Verde, Colorado, USA
The Ancestral Puebloans – Native Americans – inhabited the Mesa Verde area between 600 and 1300 CE. They were both hunter-gatherers and farmers, their agriculture consisting of maize (corn), beans and squash – termed North America's 'Holy Trinity' because the three grow well together and complement each other nutritionally.

Beginning in the 12th century, the Ancestral Puebloans began to build the 600 cliff dwellings that survive. A century later, though, prolonged droughts forced them to abandon the settlement and move further south.

OPPOSITE LEFT TOP AND BOTTOM:

Tulum, Quintana Roo, Mexico
One of the last Maya cities to
be built, Tulum, a port on the
Yucatan peninsula, reached its
peak in the 13–15th centuries. It
was an important political and
trading centre: from inland Mexico
came obsidian, gold and copper
goods, while from its coastal trade
came salt and textiles. In the early
16th century, the Spanish reached
Tulum. They challenged the Maya
on two fronts: they were both
militarily superior and they carried
with them diseases – such as
smallpox – against which the Maya
had no resistance. Within 100
years, Tulum had been abandoned.

ABOVE:

Cahokia Mounds, Illinois, USA
Built by Native Americans beside
the Mississippi River, Cahokia was
a 16 square km (six square mile)
city with rows of houses, mansions
and plazas. Archaeologists
believe that its 120 mounds, as in
Mesoamerica, were topped with
tombs, temples or palaces. Settled
around 600 CE, Cahokia became
the centre of the Mississippian
culture, of which there are traces
of satellite towns spread across the
river's flood plain. Having reached
its zenith in the 11th century,
Cahokia was abandoned 200 years
later, although historians don't
know why.

Choquequirao, Cusco, Peru
Like other sites in the Andean heartland of the Inca Empire, Choquequirao was located 3,000 metres (9,843ft) above sea level. Other than agricultural terraces, the town had temples, residences for the elite and irrigation systems to channel spring water.

OVERLEAF:
Machu Picchu, Cusco Region, Peru
Although now one of the most recognized historical sites in the world, Machu Picchu was actually settled for a relatively short time. Believed to have been built around 1450 as an estate for Inca emperor Pachacuti, it was abandoned during the Spanish conquest a century later. Although never forgotten by local people, it was unknown to the outside world until 1911.

ALL PHOTOGRAPHS:

Machu Picchu, Cusco Region, Peru

As with other Inca settlements, at Machu Picchu's highest point is a carved boulder, the Intihuatana (top), which was aligned with the winter solstice. Considering them a blasphemy, the Spanish destroyed as many Intihuatana stones as they could find.

Inca buildings were constructed of stones that were repeatedly carved until they fitted together perfectly. No mortar was used. Estimated to have housed about 750 people, there are as many as 200 houses at Machu Picchu. Many have been reconstructed.

ALL PHOTOGRAPHS:

Ollantaytambo, Cusco Region, Peru

Ollantaytambo has 17 terraces that span a dip between two promontories (bottom left). At the top of these terraces was an unfinished temple. Inca terraces were planted with potatoes, maize and quinoa (above). Livestock included llamas, alpacas and guinea pigs.

Inca settlements were established, in part, to provide shelter and sustenance for a campaigning force – Ollantaytambo meaning 'My Lord's Storehouse'. Between such settlements, the Incas built good roads to allow the army to move swiftly across the empire.

PREVIOUS PAGES:

Moray, Cusco, Peru

The circular terraces at Moray are made of stone and compacted earth. The largest circular depression is 30m (98ft) deep, and, as with other Inca sites, it has an irrigation system. Archaeologists do not know the purpose or ritual significance of these depressions.

Ollantaytambo, Cusco Region, Peru

The Spanish conquistadores arrived in Peru in 1531 with horses, some guns and, most significantly, steel swords and steel armour. Against this, the Incas had bronze or wooden clubs, slingshots, axes and only textile armour. The Spanish also carried with them a biological weapon – diseases, including smallpox. It is estimated that within a century more than 90 percent of the native population had died from disease.

And yet, at the Battle of Ollantaytambo in 1537, the Incas managed to hold off the Spanish-led troops and forced a retreat. With Spanish reinforcements approaching, however, the Incas withdrew to the forests of Vilcabamba, where Manco Inca Yupanqui founded the Neo-Inca State. This was to be the last refuge of the Inca Empire. Thirty-five years later, the Neo-Inca State fell to the Spanish.

Picture Credits